MINECRAFTER

ENGINEER

MUST-HAVE STARTER FARMS

MEGAN MILLER

Sky Pony Press
New York

Sky Pony Press books may be purchased in bulk at special discounts for sales promotion, corporate gifts, fund-raising, or educational purposes. Special editions can also be created to specifications. For details, contact the Special Sales Department, Sky Pony Press, 307 West 36th Street, 11th Floor, New York, NY 10018 or info@skyhorsepublishing.com.

Sky Pony® is a registered trademark of Skyhorse Publishing, Inc.®, a Delaware corporation.

Minecraft® is a registered trademark of Notch Development AB. The Minecraft game is copyright © Mojang AB.

Visit our website at www.skyponypress.com.

Authors, books, and more at SkyPonyPressBlog.com.

10 9 8 7 6 5 4 3 2 1

Cover and interior art by Megan Miller
Cover design by Brian Peterson
Book design by Megan Miller

Print ISBN: 978-1-5107-3256-8
E-Book ISBN: 978-1-5107-3260-5

Printed in the United States of America

CONTENTS

INTRODUCTION

DESIGNING AND ENGINEERING NEW, CREATIVE SOLUTIONS is one of the best parts of Minecraft. Farms are a great place to start! Of course, you can have plenty of fun in Minecraft without the farm designs in this guide. But if you like making ingenious contraptions or you are a bit tired of manually harvesting stacks and stacks of sugar cane to trade for emeralds, these are the starter farms to set you up very well in your early game.

Don't worry: You don't need to be a redstone expert to make these farms or understand how they work. It will all be explained! To make some of these contraptions, you will need to have mined redstone and iron and just a little quartz. But once you have a moderate supply, you are ready to tinker up some farms and reap the rewards.

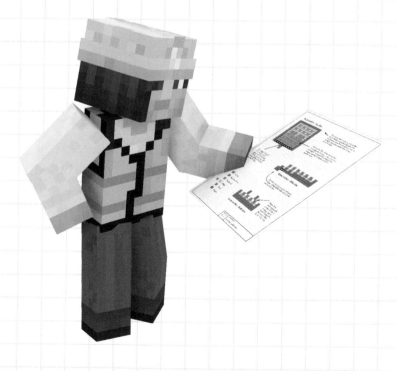

This beginner's guide also includes technical drawings and diagrams to help show where blocks go. Engineers use technical drawings, schematics, and blueprints to specify exactly where mechanisms are placed and how they are built. Two examples of how these can help: Elevations are drawings that view a model from the side, front, back, or top. Cross sections look at just a section of build, often in the middle.

Don't forget to share your Minecraft engineering accomplishments with me online. If you build any of these farms or other custom engineering designs, I'd love to see them! You, or a family member, can tweet me at @meganfmiller to showcase your work.

Smart-Start Engineering Tips —

PROTECT YOUR BUILDS! MOST REDSTONE ELEMENTS (SUCH AS REPEATERS, REDSTONE DUST, AND MORE) WILL BREAK AND FLOAT AWAY WHEN TOUCHED BY FLOWING WATER. AN ACCIDENTAL PLACEMENT OF WATER CAN WIPE OUT YOUR BUILD. WHEN YOU DO BUILD A CONTAINING STRUCTURE FOR YOUR FARMS TO PROTECT REDSTONE, MAKE SURE TO LEAVE SPACE BETWEEN YOUR REDSTONE ELEMENTS AND THE STRUCTURE. THIS STEP HELPS PREVENT PLACING BLOCKS THAT COULD INTERFERE WITH A REDSTONE SIGNAL. THE EXTRA SPACE WILL ALSO ALLOW YOU TO MOVE AROUND THE BUILD IF YOU NEED TO CHECK OR FIX LATER.

ALSO, REMEMBER TO LIGHT UP YOUR BUILDS AS YOU GO. A CREEPER IS JUST AS INTERESTED IN BLOWING UP REDSTONE AS IT IS IN DEMOLISHING YOUR BASE.

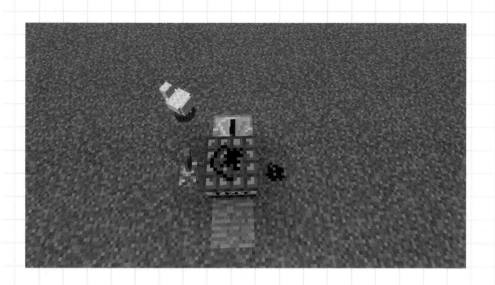

LEFT/RIGHT/FRONT/BEHIND THROUGHOUT THESE
CHAPTERS, I USE THE WORDS LEFT, RIGHT, IN FRONT,
AND BEHIND TO DESCRIBE WHERE BLOCKS ARE PLACED.
THESE DIRECTIONS ARE FROM THE POSITION OF THE
VIEWER, YOU OR ME (OR THE CAMERA), AS WE LOOK AT
THE IMAGES. SO "PLACE A BLOCK TO THE LEFT OF THE
HOPPER" MEANS TO THE LEFT OF THE HOPPER AS WE
ARE LOOKING AT IT IN THE IMAGE.

IN THE IMAGE ABOVE, THE REDSTONE IS TO THE RIGHT
OF THE TNT, AND THE LEVER IS TO THE LEFT. THE
STONE PRESSURE PLATE IS IN FRONT OF THE TNT, AND
THE REPEATER (AND THAT CHICKEN) ARE BEHIND. AND
YES, IF THE CHICKEN STEPS ON THE PRESSURE PLATE,
THE TNT WILL EXPLODE.

CHAPTER 1
SEMI-AUTOMATIC HARVESTER

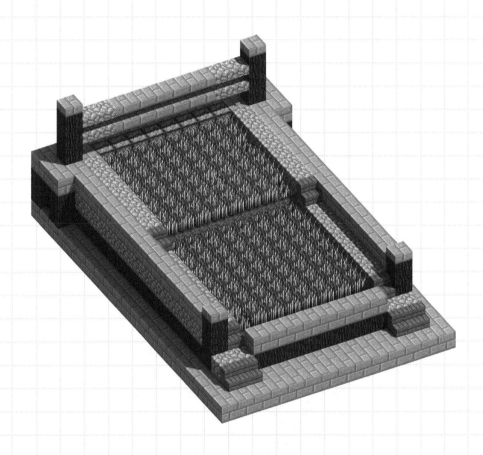

THIS EASY-TO-MAKE HARVESTER USES WATER TO BREAK your crops—wheat, carrots, potatoes, and beets—from their farmland and carry them to a chest. It's a classic contraption, often one of the first a Minecrafter builds. You can configure it to be as large as you like. The farm is staggered in platforms, or terraces, that allow a stream of water to flow down each terrace to the collection area.

How It Works

A row of dispensers is positioned above the crops. They each hold a bucket of water and are connected to a button by a line of redstone. When the crops are ready to harvest, just press the button. This simple action will send a signal down the line of redstone and activate each dispenser.

What's a Dispenser?

DISPENSERS ARE A FUNCTIONAL BLOCK THAT YOU ACTIVATE WITH A REDSTONE SIGNAL. WHEN THEY ACTIVATE, THEY EJECT ONE ITEM RANDOMLY FROM THEIR INVENTORY. DEPENDING ON THE ITEM, THEY MAY ACTUALLY PLACE OR USE THE OBJECT LIKE A PLAYER WOULD. THEY WILL FIRE ARROWS, PLACE A BOAT, AND

The dispenser looks almost identical to a dropper. The dispenser is the one that looks a little surprised.

THROW A SNOWBALL. IN THIS CONTRAPTION, THEY WILL PLACE WATER FROM A BUCKET OF WATER ON THE BLOCK IN FRONT OF THEM. WHEN THEY'RE ACTIVATED A SECOND TIME, THEY'LL USE THE EMPTY BUCKET IN THEIR INVENTORY ON THE WATER BLOCK IN FRONT OF THEM, THEREBY PICKING IT UP AND STOPPING ANY WATER FLOW.

Each dispenser will place a water source block on the block in front of it. The water will flow down the field, breaking the crops and carrying them forward. Finally, the water and crops will reach a line of hoppers. The hoppers will draw in the crops above them and transport them to a collection chest. A short time after the water is released, press the button again to have the dispensers reactivate and collect the water.

What's a Hopper?

HOPPERS TAKE ITEMS FROM A CHEST OR OTHER CONTAINER ABOVE THEM AND TRANSFER THEM TO A CHEST OR CONTAINER THEY ARE CONNECTED TO. THEY CAN EVEN TAKE ITEMS THROWN OR DEPOSITED INTO AN EMPTY BLOCK ABOVE THEM. TO POINT A HOPPER AT ANOTHER OBJECT, SHIFT-RIGHT-CLICK WITH YOUR CURSOR ON THE OBJECT YOU WANT THE HOPPER TO POINT TOWARD.

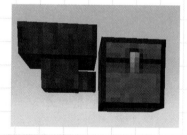

You can tell where a hopper is pointed by the bottom tube. Here, the tube is pointed toward the chest.

Step by Step

1. Build the lowest platform of dirt. It is 8 blocks long by 8 blocks wide. Refer to the technical diagram SAH-1 (page 5) as you build this farm.

2. On either side of the terrace, add a channel of water, as shown. The water channels themselves are 6 blocks long with a cobblestone border.

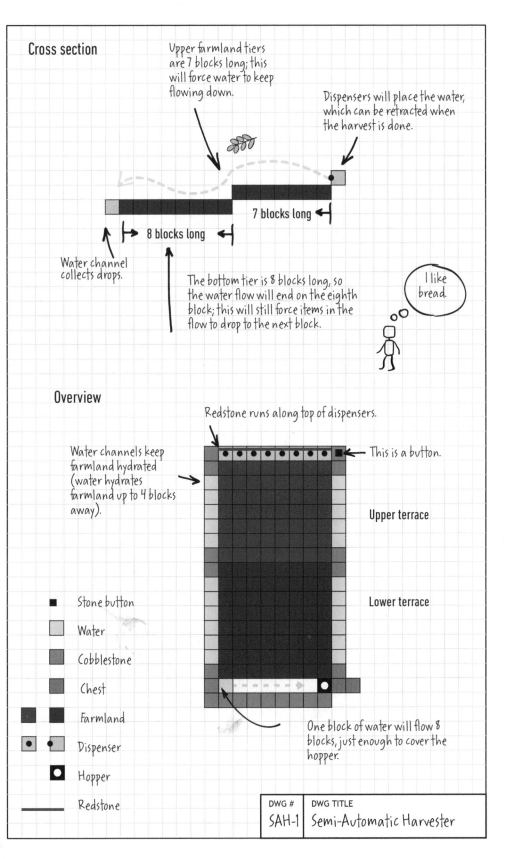

Cross section

Upper farmland tiers are 7 blocks long; this will force water to keep flowing down.

Dispensers will place the water, which can be retracted when the harvest is done.

7 blocks long

8 blocks long

Water channel collects drops.

The bottom tier is 8 blocks long, so the water flow will end on the eighth block; this will still force items in the flow to drop to the next block.

I like bread.

Overview

Redstone runs along top of dispensers.

Water channels keep farmland hydrated (water hydrates farmland up to 4 blocks away).

This is a button.

Upper terrace

Lower terrace

One block of water will flow 8 blocks, just enough to cover the hopper.

■ Stone button

☐ Water

▨ Cobblestone

▨ Chest

▨ ■ Farmland

● ● Dispenser

◉ Hopper

— Redstone

DWG #	DWG TITLE
SAH-1	Semi-Automatic Harvester

3. Now, begin to add a second terrace 1 block above the first. Start by building a platform that is as wide as the bottom terrace (including the water channels) and 7 blocks long.

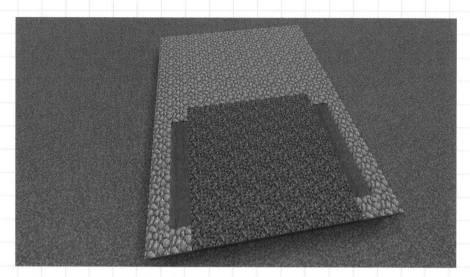

4. Then add the dirt terrace, 7 blocks long and 8 blocks wide, on the platform.

5. Add water channels on either side of this top terrace in the same way you did in Step 2. The channels will be 5 blocks long and surrounded by cobblestone (except for the dirt side).

6. Now add the water channel that will lead the harvest crops to a chest. In front of the right water channel of the bottom terrace, break a 2-block-wide hole. Inside, place a double chest.

7. Break a hole to the left of the chest. In this space, place a hopper pointed at the chest.

8. Build the water channel using cobblestone. The water will run from the leftmost dirt block to right over the hopper.

9. Add a water source at the left of the channel. It will run 8 blocks to just over the hopper.

10. Above the hopper, add a cobblestone slab. This feature will help force items flowing in the water into the hopper.

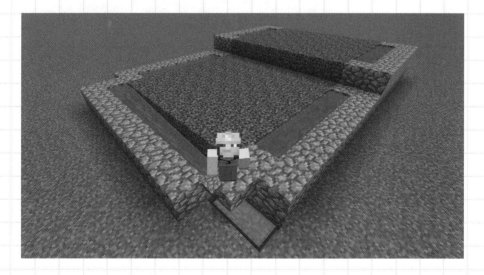

11. Behind the top terrace, add a 2-block-high wall of cobblestone.

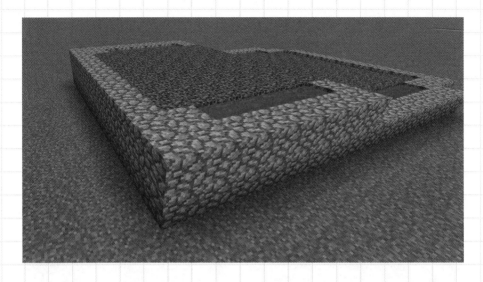

12. Place 8 dispensers on top of this wall, facing the terrace.

13. Inside each dispenser, place a bucket of water. The bucket can be in any position.

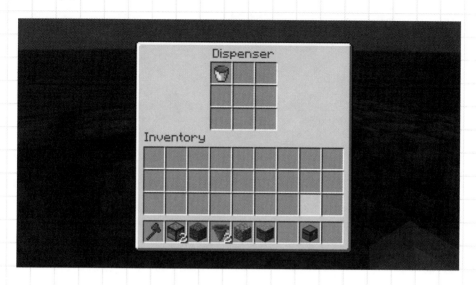

14. Add rows of cobblestone to the right and left of the dispensers. Place them over the left and right water channels, and run them to the front of the bottom terrace.

15. Place a line of redstone on top of the dispensers. On the rightmost cobblestone block, add a button.

16. Your harvester is done! All that is left now is to hoe the dirt, plant your seeds, and wait for them to grow.

17. When you are ready to harvest, press the button by the dispensers. The dispensers will all place water on the block in front of them. Wait a moment for the water to flow down your terraces. Press the button a second time to make the dispensers pick the water back up.

You'll notice that some of your crops may bounce out of the water stream. This is normal. Most of your crops will be shuttled down the bottom water channel into the hopper and into your chest. You can minimize crops hopping outside the water flow by placing higher walls around the terraces.

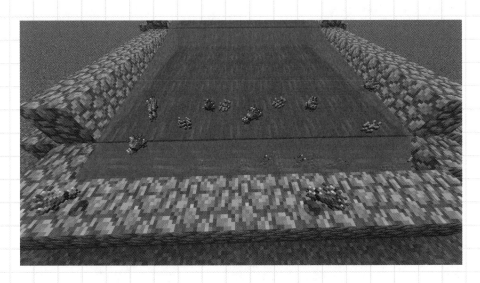

Looking for Harvest Help?

WITH THIS HARVESTER, YOU REPLANT SEEDS YOURSELF. OF COURSE, IF YOU PLACED THIS FARM WITHIN THE BOUNDS OF A VILLAGE WITH A FARMER VILLAGER, YOU MIGHT GET SOME HELP. YOU WOULD HAVE TO FIGURE OUT A WAY TO MAKE SURE THAT VILLAGERS WERE ONLY PLANTING SEEDS—NOT HARVESTING FOR THEMSELVES!

These villagers have accepted the semi-automatic harvester as one of their own farms! Just be sure to prevent them from taking any crops harvested for themselves.

Customizing Your Harvester

You can add many tiered (or stepped) terraces for a harvester following this pattern of terraces. The bottom terrace is always 8 blocks long because the water stops at the edge of the terrace. Upper terraces are 7 blocks long to make the water continue flowing down the next terrace. You can use this harvester for potatoes, beets, wheat, and carrots.

You also can decorate your harvester however you want. Replace the cobblestone with other blocks, add steps to climb up, or accent with details such as pillars and fences.

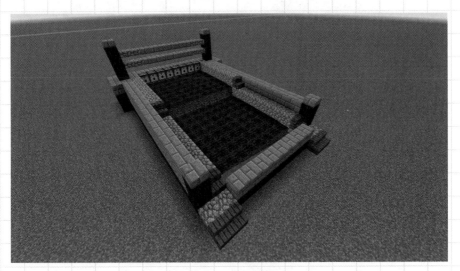

Here I added spruce pillars and stairs and raised the outer walls using stone brick. At the back, I've run some slabs over the redstone, in hopes of minimizing a water spill disaster.

CHAPTER 2
CACTUS COLLECTOR

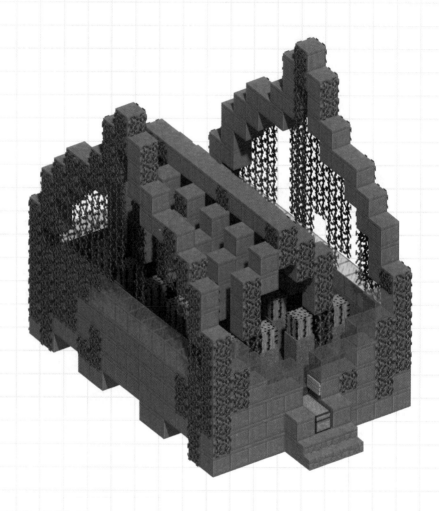

CACTUS IS HANDY FOR CREATING GREEN DYE and harming mobs. It isn't difficult to grow, but it *is* a bit annoying to try to collect. This basic cactus collection farm will break cactus automatically. Then water streams will transfer your cactus somewhere a bit less *prickly*.

How It Works

Cactus grows straight up in segments, 1 block segment at a time, like sugar cane. But it won't grow next to another block. If it tries to grow into a block that is next to another block, it breaks. This farm places blocks above growing cactus to force it to break when it grows into its second segment. Then a water stream brings the cactus to a central location for you to collect it.

Step by Step

1. Place a double chest resting on 2 building blocks of your choice. (I've chosen smooth red sandstone.) You can refer to the technical diagram CC-1 (page 18) to help you with this build.

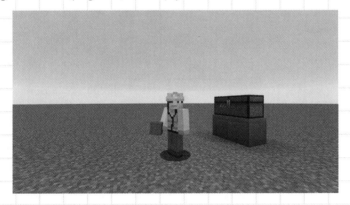

2. Now, add a hopper pointing toward the chest.

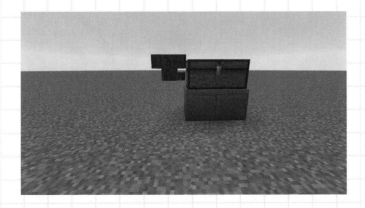

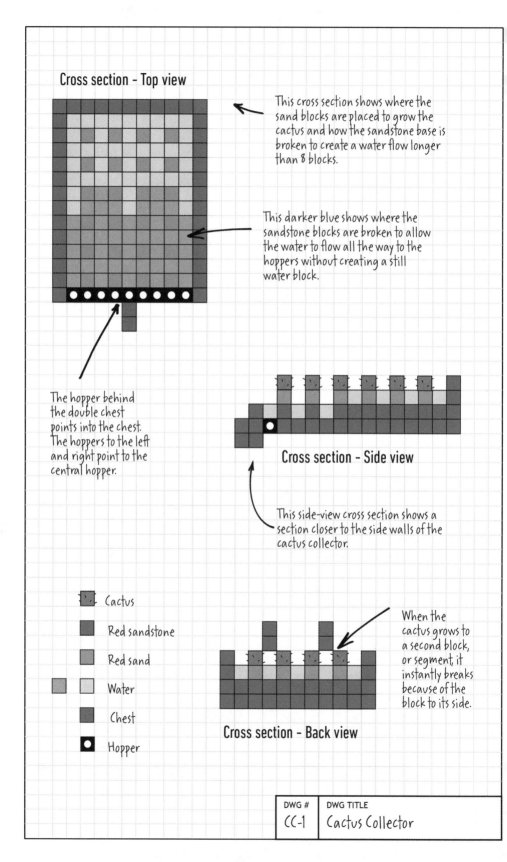

Cross section - Top view

This cross section shows where the sand blocks are placed to grow the cactus and how the sandstone base is broken to create a water flow longer than 8 blocks.

This darker blue shows where the sandstone blocks are broken to allow the water to flow all the way to the hoppers without creating a still water block.

The hopper behind the double chest points into the chest. The hoppers to the left and right point to the central hopper.

Cross section - Side view

This side-view cross section shows a section closer to the side walls of the cactus collector.

Cactus

Red sandstone

Red sand

Water

Chest

Hopper

When the cactus grows to a second block, or segment, it instantly breaks because of the block to its side.

Cross section - Back view

DWG #	DWG TITLE
CC-1	Cactus Collector

3. Add 4 hoppers to the right of the first hopper and pointing toward it.

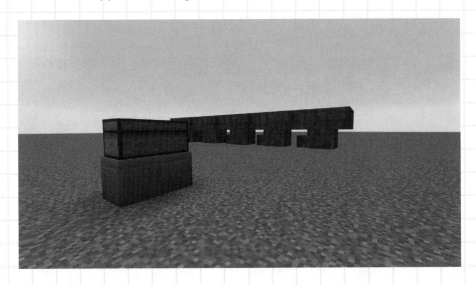

4. Add 4 more hoppers to the left of the central hopper, again pointing toward it.

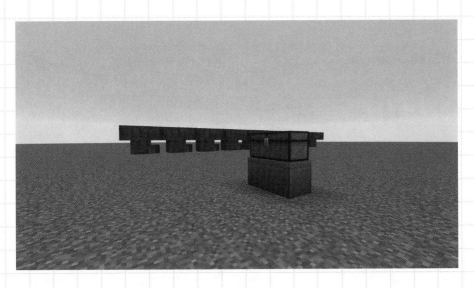

5. Next, add a 9x12 block platform, 2 blocks high, behind the row of hoppers.

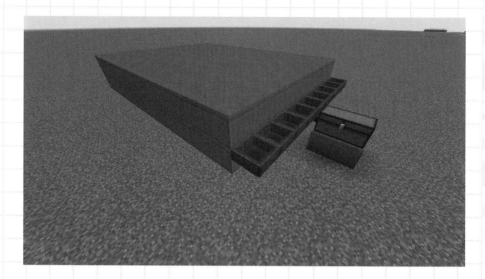

6. Add a 3-block-high wall around the platform and hoppers. The sidewalls extend 1 block beyond the hoppers.

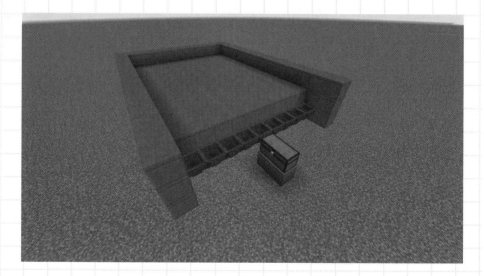

7. Add a 2-block-high wall in front of the row of hoppers.

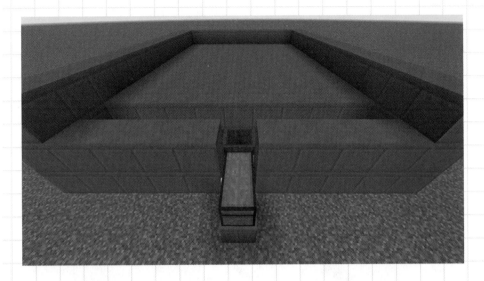

8. Place a sign above the chest next to the central hopper. This addition will stop the water flow.

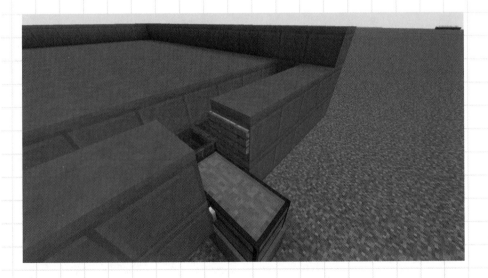

9. For the cactus to grow, place the sand in 6 rows of 4 sand each. Each block is placed 1 apart from the other, as shown.

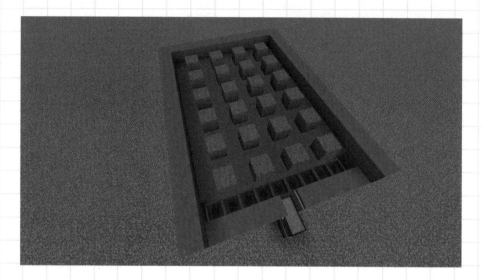

10. Now it is time to create a water flow that takes broken cactus all the way to the hopper channel. First, place a water source block at 1 back corner of the platform.

11. Place 1 more water source block at the other back corner of the platform.

12. Now place 1 final water source block in the center of the back platform, where the cursor is placed, as shown.

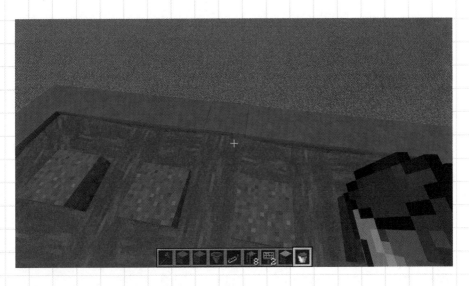

13. The image below shows how the water flow should look. We'll now break blocks that ensure the water flow reaches the hoppers without creating any standing water. We'll break the top blocks of sandstone, 1 row at a time.

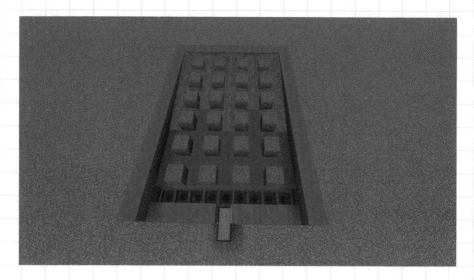

14. First, break the top blocks along the seventh row of the platform. This row is the last in which water flows across all the blocks. It's marked by the light blue wool in the image below.

15. Next, break 2 blocks in the previous row (the sixth row), marked by the yellow wool in the image below. These are the blocks to the right of the leftmost sand and to the left of the rightmost sand.

16. Going row by row, break the blocks in the 8th row through the 12th row. These are shown by the green wool (8th row), purple wool (9th row), red wool (10th row), orange wool (11th row), and lastly cyan wool (12th row), below and on pages 26 and 27.

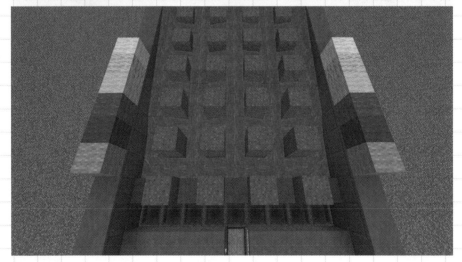

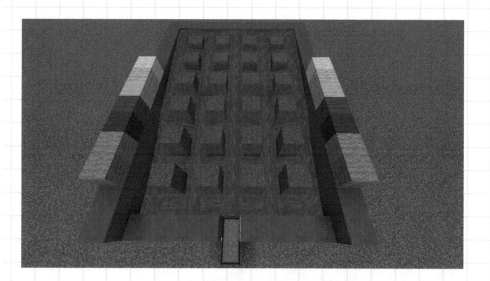

17. Place 2 strips of sandstone 2 blocks above the sand. The first strip should be centered between the 2 left long rows (front to back) of sand. The second strip should be centered between the 2 right long rows of sand.

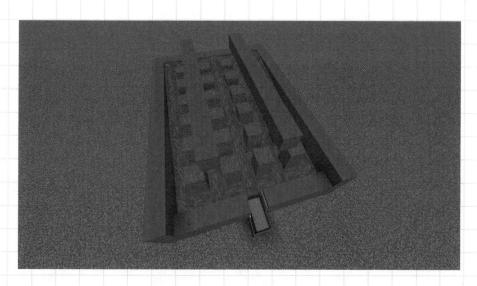

18. Break every other block of sandstone in the 2 strips, as shown. These sandstone blocks will be the cactus breakers.

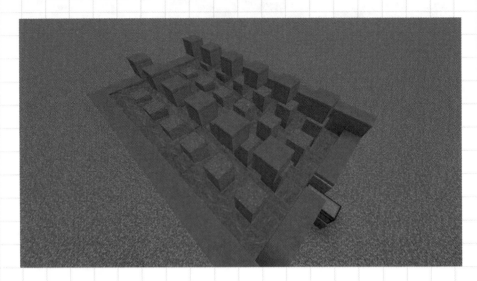

19. Add a second block above the sandstone cactus breaker blocks, so that the breakers are 2 blocks high, as shown. This addition prevents breaking cactus from landing on top of the breakers.

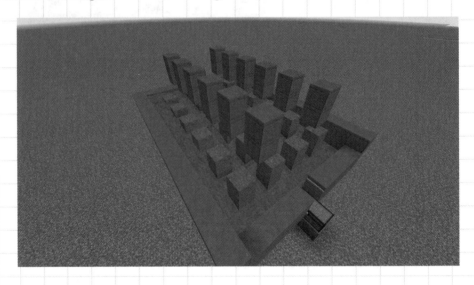

20. Now, add 1 block of cactus above every sand block.

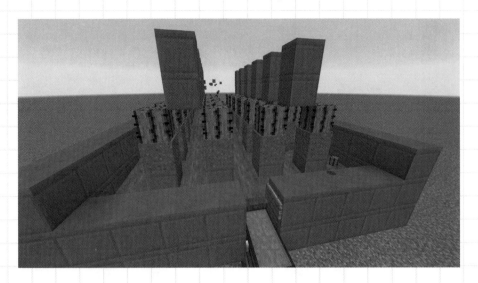

21. Build the walls around the platform up 1 block higher on the back and sides. Add additional blocks to the front wall, as shown. Your cactus farm is finished!

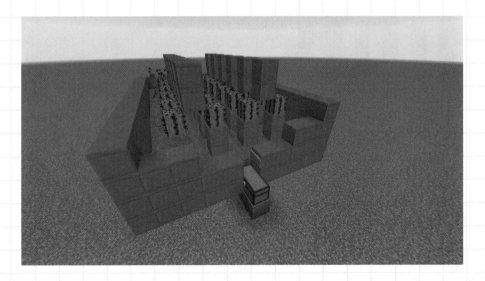

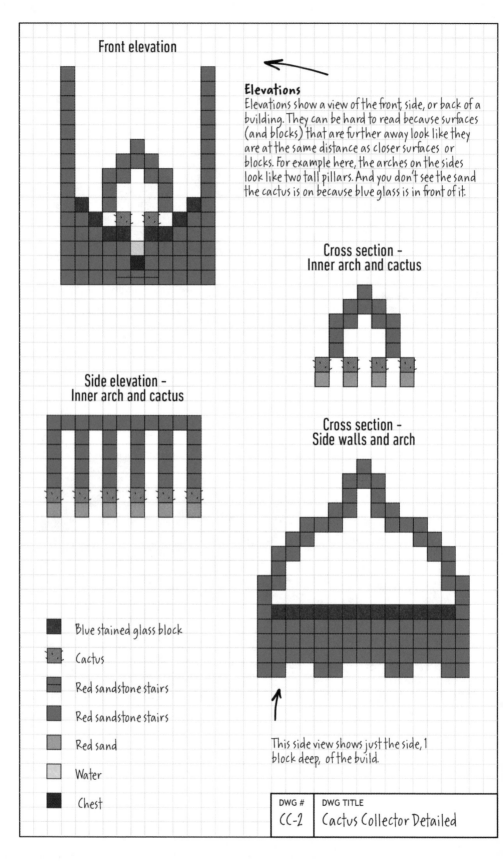

Front elevation

Elevations

Elevations show a view of the front, side, or back of a building. They can be hard to read because surfaces (and blocks) that are further away look like they are at the same distance as closer surfaces or blocks. For example here, the arches on the sides look like two tall pillars. And you don't see the sand the cactus is on because blue glass is in front of it.

Cross section – Inner arch and cactus

Side elevation – Inner arch and cactus

Cross section – Side walls and arch

Blue stained glass block

Cactus

Red sandstone stairs

Red sandstone stairs

Red sand

Water

Chest

This side view shows just the side, 1 block deep, of the build.

| DWG #
CC-2 | DWG TITLE
Cactus Collector Detailed |

Sprucing Up Your Farm

FEEL FREE TO MAKE DECORATIVE CHANGES TO YOUR
CACTUS FARM. IF YOU'D LIKE TO FOLLOW THE DESIGN
SHOWN IN THIS CHAPTER'S OPENING PICTURE, FOLLOW
THE TECHNICAL DIAGRAM CC-2 (PAGE 30). IN THE CHAPTER
OPENER BUILD, I'VE ALSO ADDED BLUE GLASS BLOCKS
TO THE TOPS OF THE WALLS AND VINES TO WIND DOWN
THE ARCHES.

CHAPTER 3
SUGAR CANE FARM

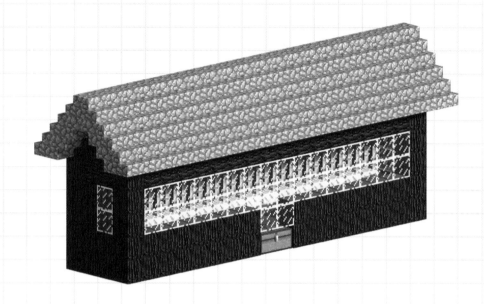

SUGAR CANE IS A MUST-HAVE FOR MAKING BOOKS for the bookshelves that surround your enchanting table. But just as important, the paper it makes can be used to trade with villagers for emeralds. And emeralds can traded for more valuable items, such as a specially enchanted sword or a cartographer's map. This sugar cane farm will hum along, producing sugar cane slowly but continually for you as you go about your other tasks and adventures.

How It Works

A row of pistons is placed behind a row of growing sugar cane, at the second block level. An observer block is placed next to a growing sugar cane, behind the location where the third block of growth would be. When the sugar cane grows from 2 blocks high to 3, the observer notices this change and emits a redstone signal out of its back. The signal is sent to the row of pistons, which activate and extend forward into the sugar cane. This breaks all of the sugar cane at the second block, leaving the first block of sugar cane to continue growing. A water channel is used to transport the broken sugar cane to hoppers, which transfer the sugar cane to chests.

What Is a Piston?

A PISTON IS A BLOCK THAT HAS A WOODEN FRONT (ITS HEAD) THAT EXTENDS WHEN GIVEN A REDSTONE SIGNAL. IT RETRACTS WHEN THE SIGNAL IS REMOVED. THE PISTON'S EXTENDED HEAD CAN MOVE MANY BLOCKS IN MINECRAFT (LIKE COBBLESTONE AND WOOD PLANKS) AND BREAK MANY OTHERS (LIKE CROPS).

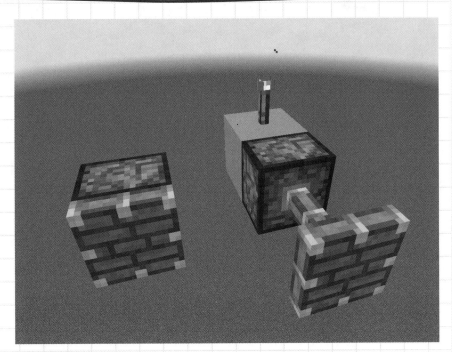

Here is a piston retracted (left) and activated with a redstone signal (right).

What Is an Observer?

AN OBSERVER BLOCK IS A REDSTONE COMPONENT THAT WATCHES THE BLOCK IN FRONT OF IT. IF THERE IS A SPECIFIC TYPE OF CHANGE, OR UPDATE, IN THAT BLOCK, IT SENDS A REDSTONE SIGNAL OUT ITS BACK. TO PLACE IT, YOU HAVE TO FACE THE DIRECTION YOU WANT THE OBSERVER TO WATCH. THE TYPES OF CHANGES AN OBSERVER CAN SEE INCLUDE PLANT GROWTH, CHESTS OPENING, PISTONS EXTENDING, AND DISPENSER ACTIVATION.

Check out the back (left) and front (right, with the eyes) of an observer block. Redstone signals are output through its "back"—the side the arrow points to. When a signal goes out, the circle on the observer's back lights up red.

Step by Step

1. Place a double chest for collecting your sugar cane. Behind it place 2 hoppers pointing into the chest. You can refer to the technical diagram SC-1 (page 36) for help in positioning blocks in this build.

2. Add 7 building blocks to the right of the right hopper and 7 blocks to the left of the left hopper, as shown. This area forms the bottom of the water channel that will transport the sugar cane to the chests. I've used oak planks.

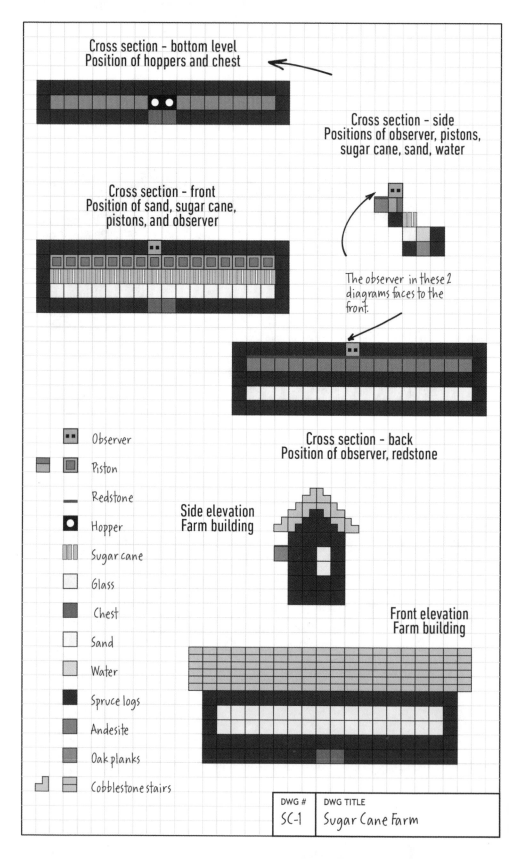

Cross section - bottom level
Position of hoppers and chest

Cross section - side
Positions of observer, pistons,
sugar cane, sand, water

Cross section - front
Position of sand, sugar cane,
pistons, and observer

The observer in these 2
diagrams faces to the
front.

Cross section - back
Position of observer, redstone

Side elevation
Farm building

Front elevation
Farm building

▪▪	Observer
▪ ▪	Piston
—	Redstone
◉	Hopper
‖‖	Sugar cane
□	Glass
▦	Chest
□	Sand
▨	Water
■	Spruce logs
▨	Andesite
▨	Oak planks
◰ ▤	Cobblestone stairs

DWG #	DWG TITLE
SC-1	Sugar Cane Farm

3. Use any building block to build a border around the oak planks and hoppers. I've used spruce logs.

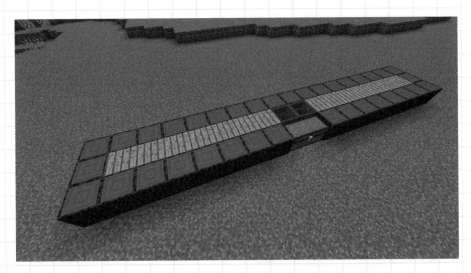

4. Above the back border, place a row of 16 sand blocks. On the sides and front, build the border up another block. Keep the double chest free, as shown.

5. Place 16 building blocks above and behind the row of sand. I've used spruce logs.

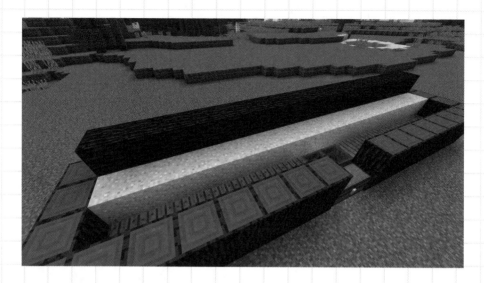

6. On this wall, just behind the sand, place 16 pistons facing out.

7. Above 1 of the central pistons, place an observer block facing out, as shown. (To place it this way, you'll need to stand behind the sand.)

8. Now finish the wall behind the sand strip so that it is as high as the observer.

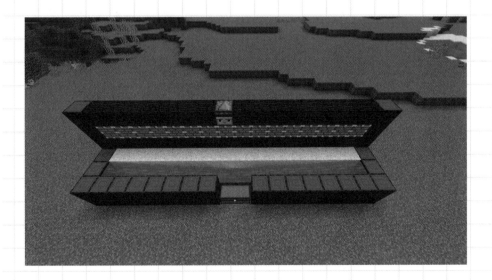

9. Behind the pistons, place a row of 16 building blocks, as shown. I've used polished andesite.

10. Add redstone all along this row. The signal from the observer block will power this line of redstone, which in turn will power the pistons.

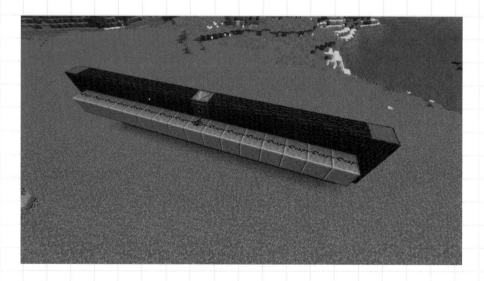

11. Place 1 water source at the far right of the water channel. The water will flow 8 blocks and stop over the right hopper.

12. Place 1 more water source block at the far left of the water channel. Now, any sugar cane falling on the right or left of the water channel will be transported to the center 2 hoppers and transferred to the double chest.

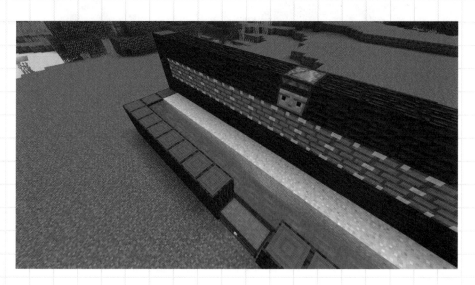

13. Plant your row of sand with 16 sugar cane.

14. Now all you have to do is build around your farm to contain breaking sugar cane and guide it into the water channel. Use glass blocks above the chest. Because they are a transparent block, they do not stop the chest from being opened.

15. Fill in a roof, walls, and sides to your farm. Use the border and back wall as the base. I've used spruce logs and glass and made a roof of cobblestone stairs.

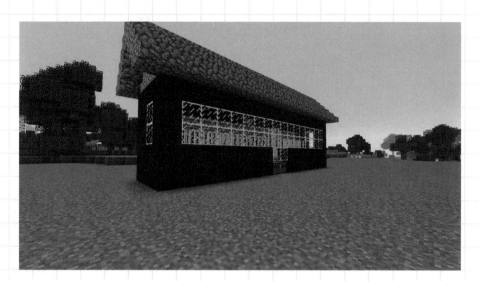

CHAPTER 4
MELON AND PUMPKIN FARMS

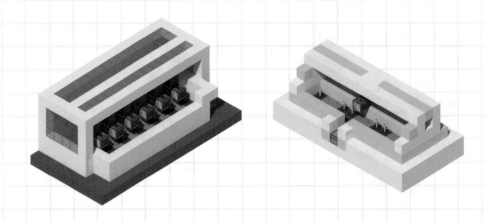

JUST LIKE SUGAR CANE, MELONS and pumpkins are great trades with villagers. Unlike wheat and other crops, you don't have to replant melons or pumpkins. Once the stalk is fully grown, it will stay to produce more melons. This means you can fully automate a melon farm.

For this build, I've given you two design options. Some players have reported a bug with the first design—the observer may activate when it shouldn't and cause repeated piston activation. Good news: The bug *should* be fixed by the time this book is published. But just to be safe, I've also included a second, more expensive (resource-wise) melon farm. I recommend starting with the cheaper farm to see if the bug is occurring on your system. In addition to the step-by-step instructions, you can refer to the technical diagram MPF-1 (page 46) for help with placing blocks.

How It Works

An observer block is placed over a block where a pumpkin or melon can grow. When the fruit grows, the observer outputs a redstone signal, which is sent to a sticky piston. The sticky piston extends, pushing the block in front of it, which breaks the melon. A series of hoppers will carry the crop to a collection chest.

What Is a Sticky Piston? —————

A STICKY PISTON IS A PISTON THAT CAN PULL AS WELL AS PUSH MANY MINECRAFT BLOCKS.

A sticky piston, retracted and extended, has a greenish slime.

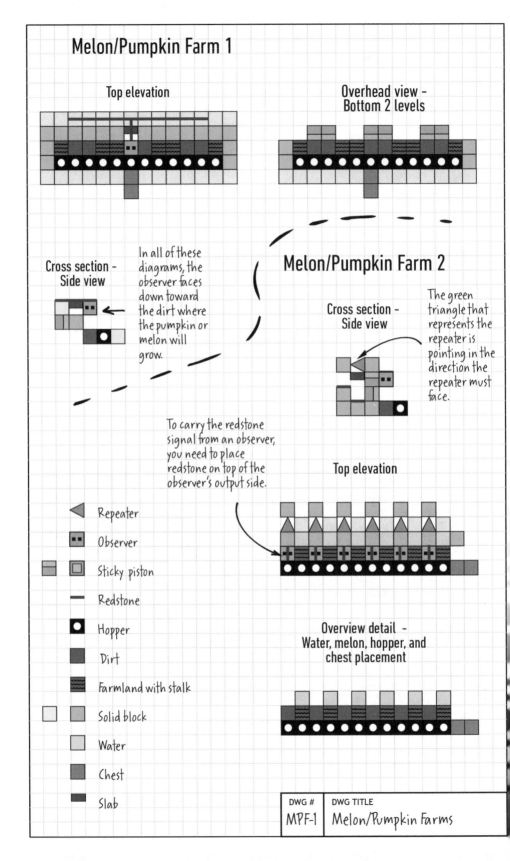

Melon/Pumpkin Farm 1

Top elevation

Overhead view – Bottom 2 levels

Cross section – Side view

In all of these diagrams, the observer faces down toward the dirt where the pumpkin or melon will grow.

Melon/Pumpkin Farm 2

Cross section – Side view

The green triangle that represents the repeater is pointing in the direction the repeater must face.

To carry the redstone signal from an observer, you need to place redstone on top of the observer's output side.

Top elevation

Overview detail – Water, melon, hopper, and chest placement

◁ Repeater

▦ Observer

▣ Sticky piston

— Redstone

◉ Hopper

▨ Dirt

▨ Farmland with stalk

▢ Solid block

▢ Water

▨ Chest

▬ Slab

DWG #	DWG TITLE
MPF-1	Melon/Pumpkin Farms

Step by Step

1. Plant 6 melon or pumpkin stalks in the 12-block-long pattern shown below. When these 12 blocks are bordered with blocks melons can't grow on, the only places melons can grow are the dirt squares shown. This pattern (2 stalks planted next to each other, with free blocks on opposite sides) prevents 2 stalks from "sharing" the same melon growth.

2. A block in front of 1 of the central 2 dirt blocks, break a 2-block-long hole for the collection chest.

3. Place the collection chest in the hole.

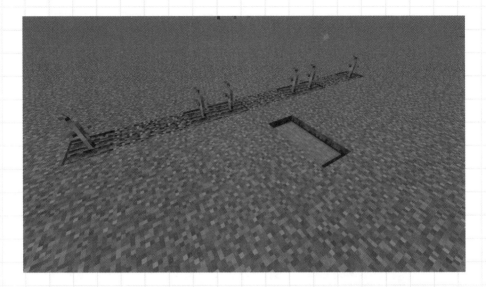

4. Dig a 12-block-long hole between the melon patch and the chest. This hole is where the hopper transport channel will go.

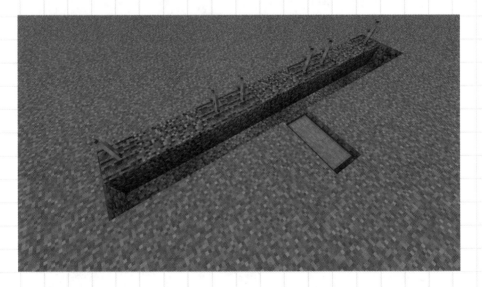

5. Place a central hopper pointing into the chest.

6. On either side of the central hopper, add a line of hoppers pointing toward that central hopper.

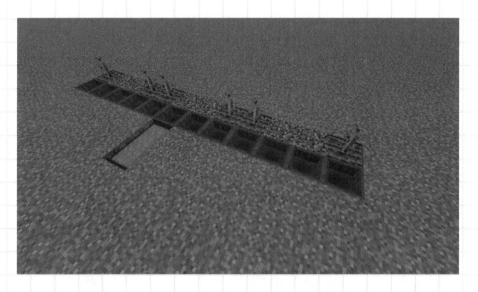

7. On the other side of the melon patch, and 1 block away, place 3 sets of 2 sticky pistons each. The pistons face toward the blocks where melons will grow.

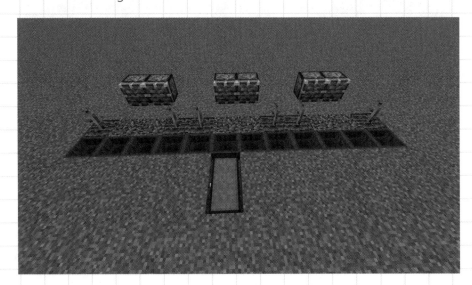

8. Place a border of building blocks between the pistons and melon patch and on the sides of the patch as well, as shown. I've used lime concrete. The pistons will push just the blocks in front of them into any grown melons.

9. Place a single block above the back border, in the center.

10. Place an observer block, facing down, against the block you placed in Step 9.

11. Run another row of blocks above the pistons, as shown. I've used yellow concrete.

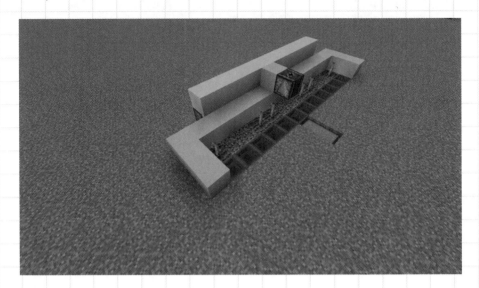

12. Run this row of blocks from the far right piston to the far left piston.

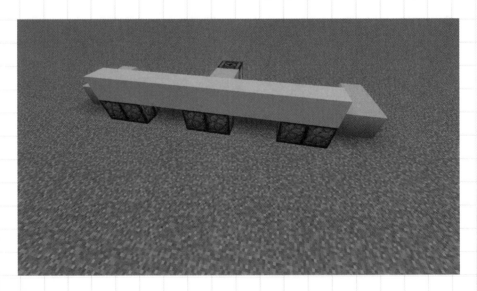

13. Now run redstone to all the blocks over the piston. Place it first on top of the observer, and then connect it to the back row of blocks.

14. Continue the back and side border around to the front, as shown. This border helps prevent broken melons from jumping away from the hopper channel. The farm is done! A flow of melons or pumpkins will begin shortly.

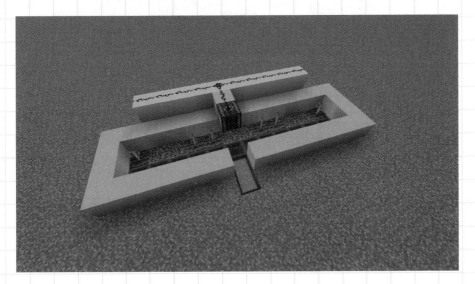

Making Simple Upgrades

THE MELONS WILL GROW FASTER IF THE FARMLAND THEY ARE ON IS HYDRATED. YOU CAN ADD BLOCKS OF WATER NEXT TO THE PISTONS, AS SHOWN.

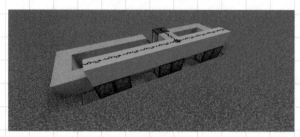

YOU CAN ADD BLOCKS OF YOUR CHOICE TO HELP BUILD A STRUCTURE AROUND THE FARM, BOTH FOR AN ARTISTIC TOUCH AND TO HELP STOP SPILLED WATER ACCIDENTS. HERE, I'VE EXTENDED THE BACK YELLOW WALL.

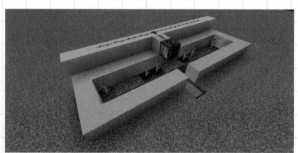

THEN I'VE ADDED A ROOF TO THE STRUCTURE USING YELLOW AND LIME CONCRETE.

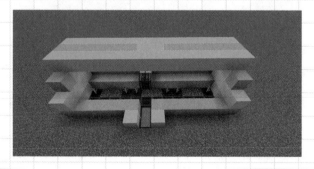

Alternate Design: Step by Step

What's the Difference?

THIS SYSTEM IS MODULAR; YOU CAN EASILY COPY AND REPEAT THE BASE PATTERN FOR 1 PUMPKIN OR MELON STALK AS MUCH AS YOU LIKE. IT USES MORE RESOURCES, INCLUDING MORE STICKY PISTONS AND REPEATERS. IT WORKS VERY MUCH LIKE THE FIRST DESIGN, EXCEPT A STICKY PISTON IS USED TO TEMPORARILY BREAK THE SIGNAL FROM THE OBSERVER. THIS FEATURE STOPS THE OBSERVER FROM REPEATEDLY REACTIVATING.

1. The base module uses 1 stalk next to 1 piece of dirt.

2. Place a building block behind the dirt, to help place a piston. Then place a piston on this block, facing forward as shown.

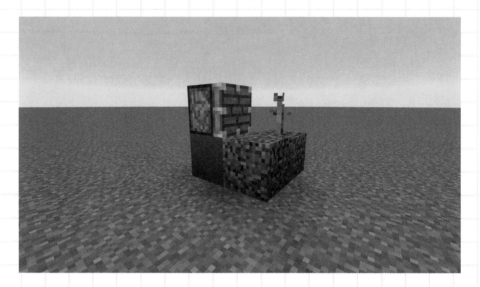

3. Place a sticky piston on top of the regular piston, facing upward.

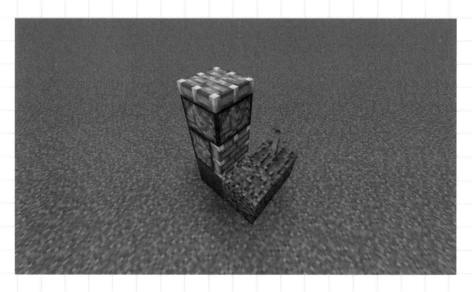

4. Place a block on top of the sticky piston.

5. Place a slab of your choice behind the sticky piston, as shown.

6. On top of the slab, place a repeater, facing backward.

What Is a Repeater?

A REPEATER IS A REDSTONE BLOCK THAT TAKES A REDSTONE SIGNAL FROM THE BACK AND OUTPUTS IT ONLY FROM ITS FRONT (IN THE DIRECTION ITS ARROW SHOWS). IT INCREASES ANY STRENGTH SIGNAL COMING IN TO A FULL-STRENGTH SIGNAL. IN ADDITION, "REDSTONE TORCH" SWITCHES ON THE REPEATER ALLOW YOU TO DELAY ITS OUTPUT SIGNAL BY 1 TO 4 TICKS.

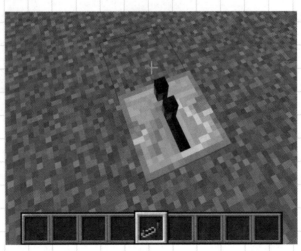

You can see a faint arrow on a repeater, pointing the direction its signal will output.

7. Place another block behind the repeater. (The repeater does face into this block.)

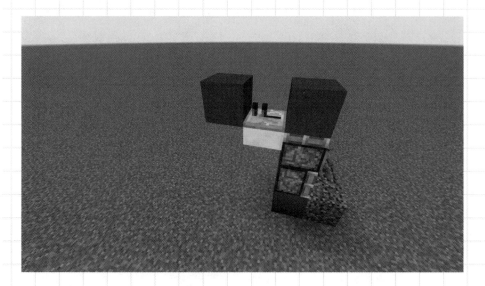

8. Place a block behind the block supporting the piston, as shown.

9. Then place a block diagonally up from that block.

10. Place redstone on the 2 blocks you just placed in Steps 8 and 9.

11. Place 1 last redstone on top of the observer. You've completed one base module. However, it doesn't have any hydration (if you want it) or a collection system.

12. Before repeating the module, first place a block behind the stalk, 1 block away. You can use the gap created later for hydrating.

13. Now, build identical copies of this module in a row, as many as you like. I've built a total of 6 here.

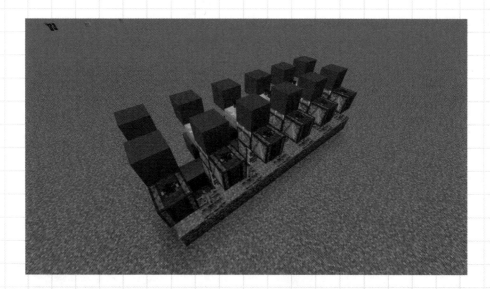

14. You can add water in the gaps left between the modules. You'll have to make a holding border for the last module, to keep the water from flowing out.

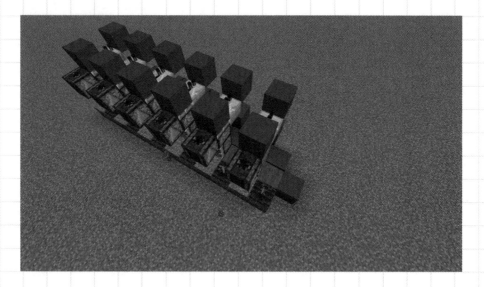

15. Now you can build a transportation system, much like the one in the first design. Place a double chest at 1 end, as shown.

16. Then run a line of hoppers pointing toward the chest.

17. Finally, add short walls around the hopper channel to assist falling melons in finding their way. And build a structure to protect your redstone from accidents. I've used yellow concrete and purple glass to finish off my structure.

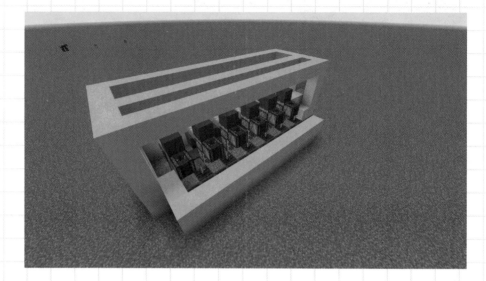

CHAPTER 5
SLIME CHUNK FARM

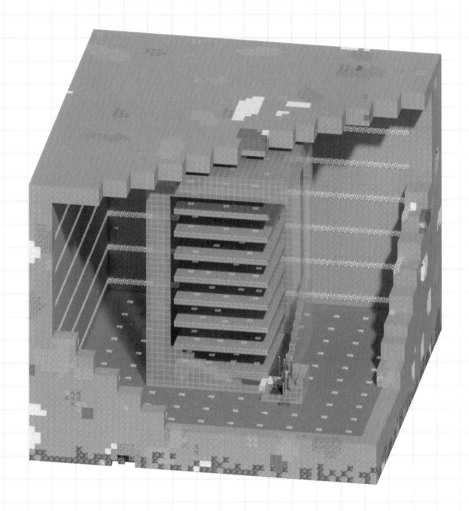

THIS SLIME FARM IS EASY BUT time-consuming to build because of its mammoth size. However, the sight of slimes bouncing to their doom is a great reward. And you will need plenty of slime balls for the sticky pistons you will use in the future.

How It Works

Slimes spawn in slime chunks on raised platforms, when you are 24 to 36 blocks away from the spawnable area. They bounce around the platform, and when they reach the edge of the platforms, they fall down to a water stream. The water stream forces them to a kill area. In this area, an iron golem stands above a single cactus. The slimes want to attack the iron golem. As they collide with the cactus in their efforts, they're damaged and killed by the cactus. Hoppers beneath collect the slimeballs.

Finding a Slime Chunk

Slime chunks are 16x16 block segments of your world, located randomly depending on the seed of your world. There's approximately 1 slime chunk for every nonslime chunk. In a slime chunk, slimes can spawn at any light below y-level 40.

By far the easiest way to find a slime chunk is to use an online slime chunk finder, like the one at chunkbase.com. Here you can enter your seed directly into the search form. You can also load the .dat file of your world.

- Click the "Load from Save" button and then browse to your Minecraft directory.

- In the folder called Saves are the different worlds you have created. Open the folder for the world you are playing and select the file with the extension ".dat".

- Once you've done this, click Search. The chunkbase app will show you the chunks that will spawn slimes.

- Note the coordinates of the chunk you want to use for your farm on in your world. Ideally, these would be close to your base, so that slimes could spawn while you are working nearby. Slimes will spawn more than 24 blocks away from you but will despawn if they are more than 36 blocks from you.

If for some reason you don't have access to a working online slime chunk locator, you can find a slime chunk yourself, although it may take a while.

- You will need to start digging out a 3-block-high space underground, at a level below y=40.

- Increase the horizontal size of the dug-out space, lighting it up until you see slimes spawning.

- Now you'll need to do some detective work to find out which chunk is spawning the slimes. Turn on chunk borders by pressing F3 and G. This function displays chunk borders in blue.

- Wall off the chunk where you think slimes are spawning, and wait until they spawn again. If they spawn outside of the walled area, test a new chunk. Keep testing until you have walled off a chunk that slimes are spawning inside. Remember, you will have to be at least 24 blocks away from a spawning area. If you are closer, slimes won't spawn even if it is a slime chunk.

Turning on chunk borders will show blue, yellow, and red lines. The blue lines show the chunk you are in. The yellow ones are spaced every 2 blocks. The red lines show the borders of adjacent chunks. If you look up, you'll see blue lines showing every 16-block vertical segment of the chunk you are in.

Step by Step

1. When you've found your slime chunk, your goal is to dig out the chunk, along with an additional 3-block space on all sides. The 3-block-wide gaps on all sides of the platforms allow the slimes to fall down. This means the total dig space is a 22x22-block wide area, centered on your chunk from y=11 to y=42. You can make this space less high if you decide on fewer platforms. You can have fewer platforms, but you should have at least 4. Fewer platforms will decrease the spawning rate.

Refer to the technical diagram SCF-1 (page 72) for a cross section of this slime chunk farm. The diagram is based on having the maximum number of spawning platforms between y=11 and y=39. Notice that each platform leaves a 3-block space between it and the lower platform to allow the biggest slimes to spawn.

Dig out the area in a way that suits you best. For example, you can dig out your slime chunk entirely and build platforms as you go. You can wait to build the platforms after you've dug out your chunk. You could also just dig out the spaces between the platform levels.

Light up by embedding Jack O' Lanterns in the platforms. The light will prevent other mob types from spawning. It also maximizes the spawning space on each platform by avoiding torches or glowstone, which is not seen as a solid block.

The 22x22 area is dug out, from y=11 through y=42.

The second platform is complete.

The eighth and final platform is complete.

Increasing Spawn Rates

TO GET THE MAXIMUM NUMBER OF SPAWN RATES FOR YOUR FARM, YOU WILL WANT AS MANY PLATFORMS AS POSSIBLE. SOMETIMES YOU CAN FIND SEVERAL SLIME CHUNKS NEXT TO EACH OTHER. FIGURE ON DOUBLE THE DIGGING THOUGH!

A BIG FACTOR IN IMPROVING SLIME RATES IS LIGHTING UP THE AREA AROUND YOU. LIGHT UP CAVES AND THE SURFACE IN A 128-BLOCK RADIUS AROUND THE FARM. THE LIGHT PREVENTS OTHER MOBS FROM SPAWNING AND LIMITS THE TOTAL NUMBER OF MOBS THAT CAN SPAWN AROUND YOU. IF YOU LIGHT UP THIS AREA, YOU WILL HAVE A GREAT SPAWN RATE AND MORE SLIME THAN YOU WILL KNOW WHAT TO DO WITH!

---

2. Once your platforms are in place, with a 3-block space around all sides, dig a 2-block deep and 3-block wide channel around the bottom platform. This area is where the slimes will fall and be pushed by the water into the kill area.

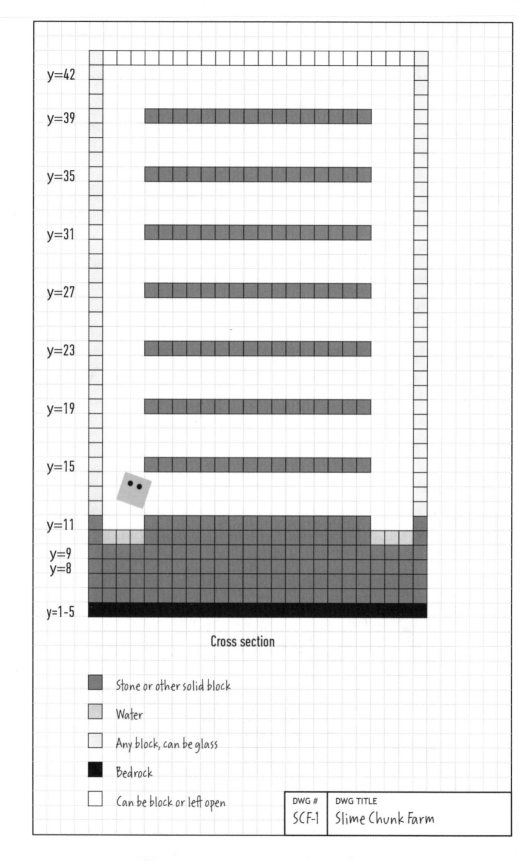

Cross section

Stone or other solid block

Water

Any block, can be glass

Bedrock

Can be block or left open

DWG #	DWG TITLE
SCF-1	Slime Chunk Farm

3. Starting at the corner opposite to where you want the kill area to be, place 3 water source blocks along 1 outer wall, as shown.

4. Continue the water flow along the channel by doing the following: On the last 3 blocks of the water flow, place 3 signs on the channel floor, as shown.

5. Add 3 more source blocks of water on the other side of the stopped water flow.

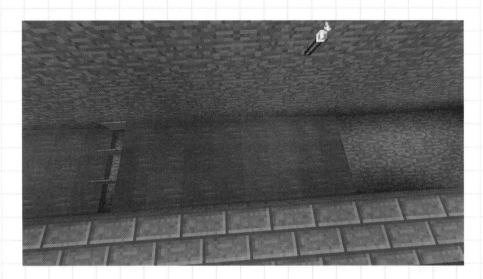

6. Repeat Steps 4 and 5 until the water flow reaches the opposite corner from where you started. Do the same for the other side of the channel, so that wherever a slime falls, it will be pushed to the kill area.

7. Now, construct the kill area, shown in the technical diagram SCF-2 (page 76). It is a 5 wide x 5 long x 8 high space that juts 2 blocks into the main 22x22 area, at 1 corner.

8. Place temporary sand blocks to stop the water flow while you are working. Break the bottom floor blocks in this 5x5 area.

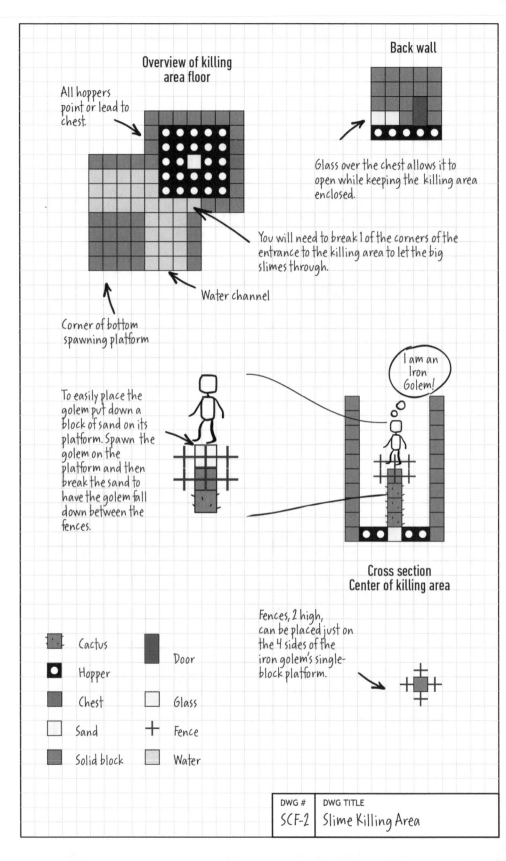

Overview of killing area floor

Back wall

All hoppers point or lead to chest.

Glass over the chest allows it to open while keeping the killing area enclosed.

You will need to break 1 of the corners of the entrance to the killing area to let the big slimes through.

Water channel

Corner of bottom spawning platform

To easily place the golem put down a block of sand on its platform. Spawn the golem on the platform and then break the sand to have the golem fall down between the fences.

I am an Iron Golem!

Cross section Center of killing area

Fences, 2 high, can be placed just on the 4 sides of the iron golem's single-block platform.

Cactus

Hopper

Chest

Sand

Solid block

Door

Glass

Fence

Water

DWG #
SCF-2

DWG TITLE
Slime Killing Area

9. Place a double chest at the border of 1 wall of the kill area. Place 2 glass blocks above it. This addition allows the chest to open and keeps the walls intact. Build a room on the other side of the chest. This room will be the permanent access to your slime chest, so you will want to create a way to get there from the outside or a nearby cave.

10. Place 24 hoppers, pointing to the double chest in the 5x5 kill area, so that any dropped slimeballs will make their way to the chest. Leave the central block open.

11. At the center of the 5x5 area, place 1 block of sand with 3 cactus blocks above it.

12. Above the top cactus block, place any solid block. I've used polished andesite. This platform will hold the iron golem.

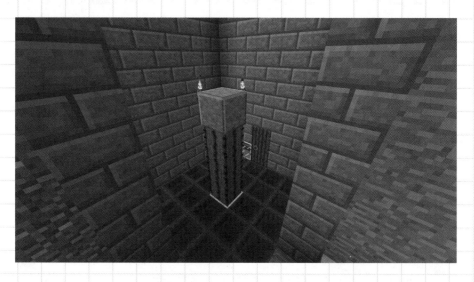

13. Place fences around the golem's platform as shown, using 8 fences, 2 on each side.

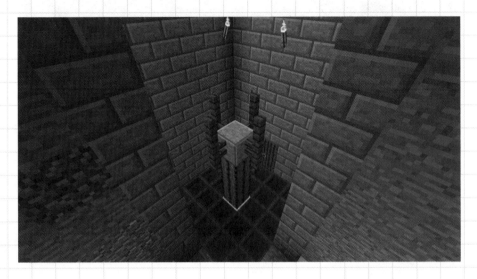

14. Place 1 block of sand on top of the platform.

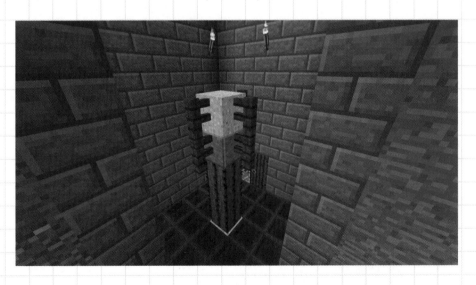

15. On top of the sand, place the 4 iron blocks to create the iron golem.

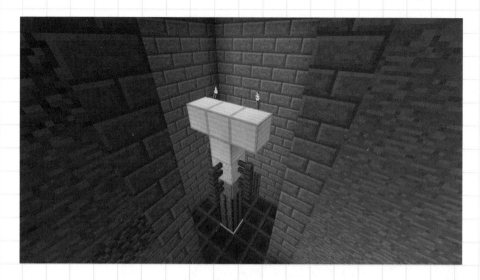

16. When you are ready, place the pumpkin on top of the middle iron block. This step will instantly create the golem.

17. Now, quickly break the sand block, so the iron golem falls down a block onto the platform. You're done!

Detailing Your Slime Farm

YOU CAN DETAIL YOUR SLIME FARM AS YOU LIKE.
(REMEMBER TO BREAK ANY SAND BLOCKING THE WATER
CHANNEL FLOW.) AS YOU CAN SEE FROM THE CHAPTER
OPENER IMAGE (PAGE 65), I'VE MADE AN EVEN BIGGER
SPACE HERE IN WHICH TO HOUSE THE SLIME CHUNK FARM.
I'VE USED LIGHT BLUE GLASS TO BORDER THE 22x22
SLIME FARM, SO I CAN SEE THE POOR SLIMES HOPPING TO
THEIR DOOM.

CHAPTER 6
MONSTER SPAWNER
XP FARM

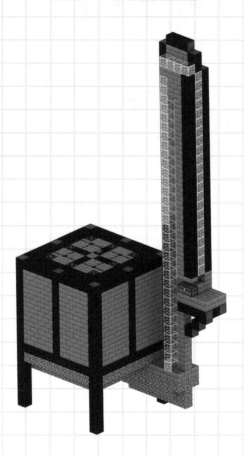

WHEN YOU FIND A DUNGEON with a spawner, don't destroy the spawner! After "Don't dig straight down" and "Don't dig straight up," this is a cardinal rule for advanced survival play. A mob spawner can be the source of bushels of drops to trade with villagers or endless XP to help you enchant your gear at the highest levels.

An XP farm is a farm that gathers mobs in an area where you can safely kill them and gather those green glowing orbs of experience. It will also have a way to gather any loot the mob drops. This monster spawner XP farm is a classic, and you can use it for skeletons or zombie spawners. It doesn't require many resources, so you can build one in your early game.

How It Works

Given the monster spawner rules (see "Understanding Spawners," page 86), we need to build a farm that does the following:

- Allows for as large a dark spawning area as possible

- Gets the mobs out of the 9x9x9, 6-mob-max area as fast as possible

- Places the mobs in a location where the player is within 16 blocks of the spawner

In this spawner farm, we create a 9x9x5 spawning area. Water will flush the mobs out of the 9x9x9 area.

The design uses water to push the mobs to a water elevator. The elevator brings the mobs up to a specific height and then forces them to fall to their near death. The goal is to have the mobs take so much fall damage that you can kill them with 1 punch. Using a mechanism to damage mobs before you kill them is often called "softening" them. Other softening methods include using pistons to squish them (suffocate, really) or using lava to burn them.

Creative Spawners

YOU CAN'T PICK UP AND MOVE THE SPAWNERS YOU FIND IN VANILLA MINECRAFT. HOWEVER, YOU CAN CREATE NEW MOB SPAWNERS IN CREATIVE MODE. IN CREATIVE MODE, YOU CAN GIVE YOURSELF A SPAWNER WITH THE COMMAND:

/GIVE (YOUR USERNAME) mob_spawner.

THIS COMMAND GIVES YOU A GENERIC PIG SPAWNER. TO CHANGE THE TYPE OF MOB IT SPAWNS, FIRST SELECT A SPAWN EGG FOR ANY MOB IN YOUR CREATIVE INVENTORY. THEN RIGHT-CLICK THE SPAWNER TO CHANGE ITS MOB.

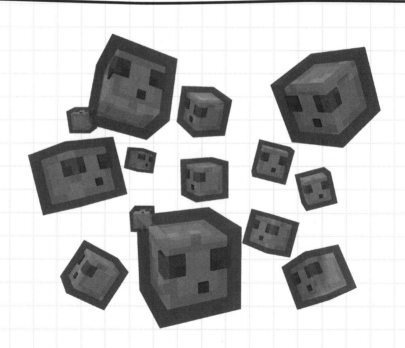

The generic creative mode spawner is a pig spawner. The type of mob that a spawner generates rotates in the center of the spawner cage.

Step by Step

1. First light up the area around your spawner to stop it from activating! Torches on the top and sides of the spawner and a few on the dungeon walls should be enough. Light up and close off any cave area that is next to the dungeon so you can work safely.

2. Clear out the area around your spawner. You should clear a spawning area that is 9x9x5, centered on the spawner. Refer to the technical drawing XP-1 (page 87) for help with the exact placement of any blocks and features.

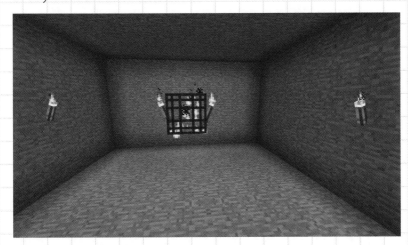

Understanding Spawners

VANILLA MONSTER SPAWNERS FOLLOW SPECIFIC RULES TO
SPAWN THEIR MOBS. OVERALL:

1. A SPAWNER IS ONLY ACTIVATED WHEN A PLAYER IS
WITHIN 16 BLOCKS.

2. A SPAWNER CAN ONLY SPAWN THEIR DESIGNATED
MOB IN A 9X9 AREA (2.5-4 BLOCKS HIGH) CENTERED
ON THE SPAWNER. THE PRECISE AREA VARIES
VERY SLIGHTLY FOR EACH MOB, FROM 8.3X8.3 TO
9.4X9.4. MOBS ARE MORE LIKELY TO SPAWN CLOSER
TO THE SPAWNER THAN FARTHER. OVERALL, A
9X9X5 CLEARED SPAWNING AREA (CENTERED ON
THE SPAWNER) WILL WORK WELL FOR VANILLA
MINECRAFT MOB TRAPS.

3. THE SPAWNER MOBS CAN SPAWN IN THE AIR
(UNLIKE REGULAR MOB SPAWNING RULES, WHERE
THEY NEED SOLID BLOCKS TO STAND). THE SPAWN
LOCATION MUST BE DARK ENOUGH (LIGHT LEVEL 7
OR BELOW) AND FREE OF SOLID BLOCKS.

4. THE SPAWNER WILL TRY TO SPAWN 4 MOBS IN
RANDOM LOCATIONS WITHIN THE SPAWN AREA. IF IT
DOESN'T FIND A SPAWNABLE AREA FOR EVEN 1 MOB
WITH ITS FIRST TRY, IT KEEPS TRYING UNTIL
IT IS SUCCESSFUL. ONCE IT IS SUCCESSFUL, THE
SPAWNER WAITS FOR A COOLDOWN PERIOD (10-40
SECONDS) BEFORE TRYING AGAIN. WHEN IT SPAWNS

THE MOBS, THE SPAWNER PRODUCES A LARGE PUFF OF WHITE SMOKE PARTICLES.

5. IF THERE ARE 6 MOBS ALREADY WITHIN A 9x9x9 BLOCK AREA, CENTERED ON SPAWNER, THE SPAWNER WILL STILL MAKE THE SPAWNING ANIMATION BUT NOT SPAWN ANY MORE MOBS. IT WILL WAIT THROUGH ITS COOLDOWN PERIOD BEFORE TRYING AGAIN.

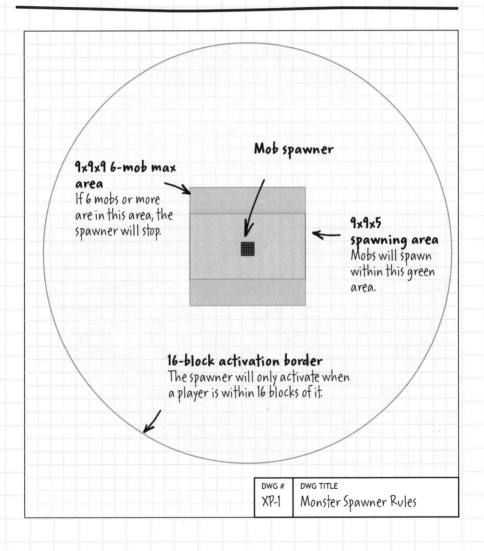

Mob spawner

9x9x9 6-mob max area
If 6 mobs or more are in this area, the spawner will stop.

9x9x5 spawning area
Mobs will spawn within this green area.

16-block activation border
The spawner will only activate when a player is within 16 blocks of it.

DWG #	DWG TITLE
XP-1	Monster Spawner Rules

3. Along the back wall, place 2 buckets of water in 2 corners.

4. Break the 9 blocks in the floor that are the last blocks that the flow of water hits. This will let the water flow for longer than 8 blocks, all the way to the front of the spawning chamber.

Custom Spawners

YOU CAN ALSO USE COMMAND BLOCKS TO CREATE CUSTOM SPAWNERS—WITH CUSTOM MOBS, SPAWNING AREAS AND RATES, AND MORE. TO HELP CREATE THE COMMAND FOR YOUR COMMAND BLOCK, YOU CAN VISIT ONE OF A NUMBER OF WEBSITES THAT HELP CUSTOMIZE COMMANDS, LIKE THE MINECRAFTUPDATES.COM SUMMON COMMAND TOOL.

---

5. Now break the blocks between the ones you broke in Step 4 and the front of the chamber.

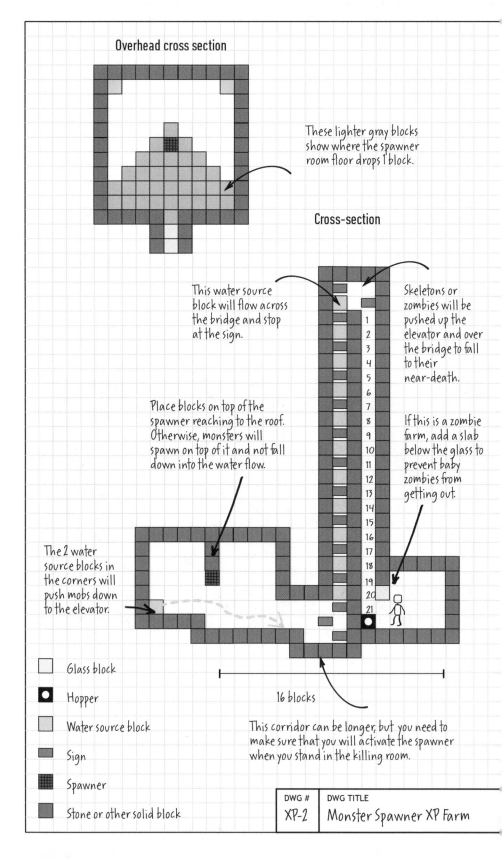

Overhead cross section

These lighter gray blocks show where the spawner room floor drops 1 block.

Cross-section

This water source block will flow across the bridge and stop at the sign.

Skeletons or zombies will be pushed up the elevator and over the bridge to fall to their near-death.

Place blocks on top of the spawner reaching to the roof. Otherwise, monsters will spawn on top of it and not fall down into the water flow.

If this is a zombie farm, add a slab below the glass to prevent baby zombies from getting out.

The 2 water source blocks in the corners will push mobs down to the elevator.

1	
2	
3	
4	
5	
6	
7	
8	
9	
10	
11	
12	
13	
14	
15	
16	
17	
18	
19	
20	
21	

☐ Glass block

◉ Hopper

☐ Water source block

☐ Sign

▒ Spawner

☐ Stone or other solid block

16 blocks

This corridor can be longer, but you need to make sure that you will activate the spawner when you stand in the killing room.

DWG #	DWG TITLE
XP-2	Monster Spawner XP Farm

6. In the center of the front wall, break open a corridor that is 1 block wide, 3 blocks high, and at most 9 blocks long. As you create the corridor, you can see the water flow from the back walls stops 2 blocks into the corridor. Break the last block the water is on to let the water flow continue. Then break blocks along the rest of the floor of the corridor, so that the water flows to the end of the corridor.

7. At the end of this corridor create a 3x3 room. This will be the killing chamber, a room where you will stand to kill the mobs after they drop. You will need a way to exit and enter the killing chamber from the cave where you discovered the spawner, or from the outside. Build that now, if you haven't already.

8. Place a temporary block at the beginning of the corridor (by the spawning room) to stop water flow and make it easier to work.

9. The bottom of the elevator will be 2 blocks in (toward the spawner). Replace the floor block here with something to mark the spot, like a stone brick block or a bright concrete block.

10. The next block down the corridor (away from the spawner) is the block over which (at the top of the elevator shaft) the mobs will travel to their fall. Place a block here to show this area will later be a wall up to the top of the elevator shaft. I've used a mossy stone brick block.

11. If necessary, place a block between the block you placed in Step 10 and the killing room so that this is now level with the killing chamber.

12. To collect the skeleton drops, we'll use a hopper and a chest. First break a 2-block-high, 2-block-wide space to the side of the corridor to fit a double chest.

13. Place a hopper next to the chest, pointing into it. This is what the skeletons will drop down on.

14. Place 2 slabs above the chest.

15. Now it's time to dig out the drop shaft (above the hopper) and the elevator shaft that pulls the skeletons up. Refer to the technical diagram XP-2 (page 90) to see how they are placed. There are many ways to dig out or build these tunnels. For example, you could use temporary ladders to climb up, or sand to pillar up.

As you can see on the diagram, the drop shaft should be 21 blocks higher than the hopper, not 22. The reason: Some of the skeletons jump upward in the water that is pushing them to the drop. This jump can add a block's worth of damage to their fall, which can kill them. A 21-block drop will leave skeletons alive, with either 1 or .5 points of health. (Of course, any skeletons that fall with armor have more protection, and will have more health after the drop.)

Fall Damage

MOBS THAT CAN TAKE FALL DAMAGE WILL ONLY START
TAKING FALL DAMAGE WITH THE FOURTH BLOCK OF
FALLING. THAT MEANS, ONCE THEY'VE FALLEN 3 BLOCKS,
THEY (AND YOU!) WILL TAKE 1 HEALTH POINT (HP) OR A
HALF HEART OF DAMAGE FOR EACH NEXT BLOCK. SKELETONS
AND ZOMBIES EACH HAVE 20 HP (10 HEARTS). TO GET THEM
DOWN TO 1 HP, OR HALF A HEART, THEY'LL NEED TO FALL
19 BLOCKS AFTER THE FIRST 3, OR A TOTAL OF 22 (19 +3)
BLOCKS. THEORETICALLY.

---

16. Once the 2 shafts are built (along with the wall separating the two),
you need to place the water that will push the skeletons up the
elevator and over to the drop shaft. At the bottom of the elevator
shaft, place 3 signs as shown, on a sidewall.

17. Place a water block between the 2 signs at the back. The water is contained by the 3 signs.

18. Now, going up the elevator, place a sign every other block and water between the signs. Do this until you reach the top bridge. At the top, place a sign at what will be the skeleton's head level on the elevator side. On the drop side, place a sign just above the drop, as shown.

19. Now, place water between the 2 top signs of the elevator shaft. This water will push the skeletons over to the drop shaft.

20. Back down in the killing chamber, block off the area where the skeletons will fall so just their lower halves of their bodies are exposed—and they can't get out! Here, I've placed a glass block in front of the drop shaft.

21. Your XP farm is ready to go! Remove any extra ladders, torches, and other temporary building materials. Make sure the spawning chamber is fully dark, and then get back to the killing chamber. You should be able to kill armorless skeletons with a bare-fisted punch or two. You may want to use a stone sword if you get a lot of armored skeletons.

CHAPTER 7
AUTOMATIC CHICKEN COOKER

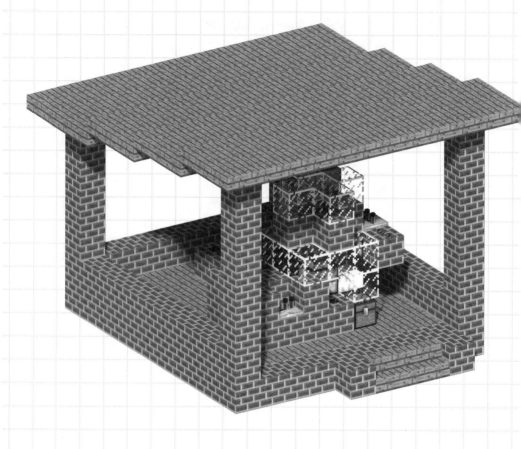

NOT A MINECRAFT VEGETARIAN? AN AUTOMATIC chicken farm is hands-down the best way to get a constant supply of high-saturation food with very little effort. Once you've set up the contraption and added enough chickens, there's nothing else you need to do—except get your roast chicken and eat it, too.

How It Works

Chickens are contained in a single-block space. They lay eggs that a hopper picks up and transfers to a dispenser. The dispenser throws the eggs into another area, where some of them hatch into baby chicks. Above the baby chicks' heads is another dispenser that flares out lava every so often. Because the baby chicks are smaller than the lava spurt, the lava misses them. However, when a chick grows into a chicken, it is big enough to be killed by the lava spurt. It drops cooked chicken and maybe a feather or two. The cooked chicken and feathers are collected by another hopper and transferred to a chest.

Step by Step

1. First, place the chest where the cooked chicken will collect. Add a hopper behind this and pointing into it.

2. To the left of the hopper, place a block (see "Best Block Choices," below) on the ground and a dispenser pointing toward the hopper. This dispenser will throw the eggs to make the chicks that will grow up to become roast chicken.

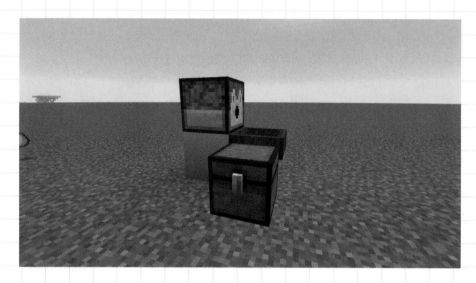

Best Block Choices

BECAUSE LAVA IS INVOLVED IN THIS BUILD, USE A LAVA-PROOF BLOCK SUCH AS STONE, BRICK, OR CONCRETE. IF YOU USE WOOL, YOU WON'T HAVE A CHICKEN COOKER FOR VERY LONG! BY THE WAY, THE CHICKENS IN THIS CHAPTER'S IMAGES ARE ALL ESCAPEES FROM ANOTHER CHICKEN FARM THAT WENT UP IN FLAMES.

3. Place a slab on top of the hopper. The slab allows the dispenser to throw eggs into it, and any chicks to hatch above. Without this, the thrown eggs will hurt any chicks living right on top of the hopper. The hopper below will still gather any drops that collect on top of the slab.

4. Add a hopper on top of the dispenser. This hopper will collect the eggs from the egg-laying chickens, who will live right on top of the hopper.

5. Now we need to make the dispenser activate whenever an egg is dropped into it. Otherwise, the eggs will just collect in the dispenser. To do this, we need to send the dispenser a redstone signal for every egg that comes into it. First, place a block to the left of the dispenser and a comparator on top of this block. The comparator must face away from the dispenser. You'll see a faint arrow on the comparator, pointing in the direction it is facing. The comparator will detect when objects are in the dispenser's inventory and send a signal out its front end. Add a stack of 16 test eggs inside the dispenser, and you will see the comparator light up.

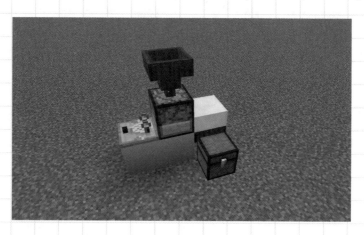

6. Add 2 blocks, stacked, to the left of the comparator. (The bottom block isn't necessary, but is helpful to place the top block.)

7. Then add another block to the left of the 2 stacked blocks. Place 1 redstone on top of this single block. It will light up, because the signal from the comparator passes through the block to the redstone.

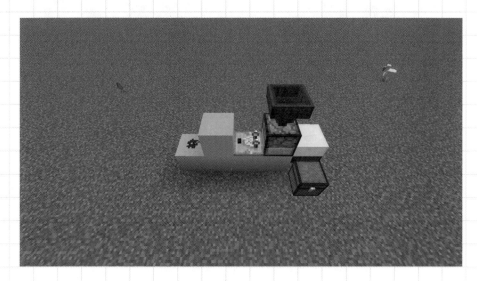

8. Add a stack of 2 blocks in front of the single block placed in Step 7.

9. Add another block to the right of the second stack of blocks. Place a repeater, facing right (back toward the comparator), on top of it.

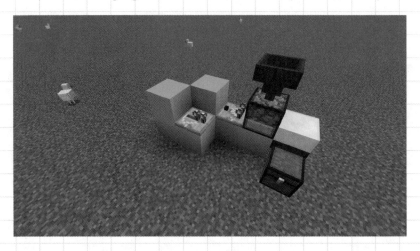

10. Place another stack of 2 blocks to the right of the repeater and a single block to the right of these, as shown. On top of the single block, place 1 redstone. This redstone will take the signal from the block powered by the repeater and send it to the dispenser.

The redstone will light up, activate the dispenser, and throw an egg into the slab. However, you will still have 15 eggs in the dispenser. The dispenser performs only one action per signal.

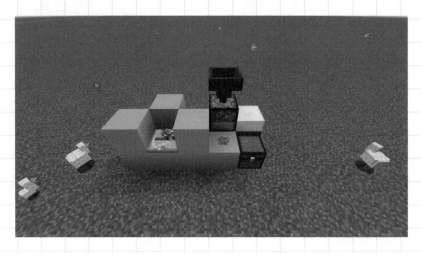

11. Our next goal is to keep the dispenser activating as long as there are any eggs in it. First, we'll move to view the contraption from what is currently the back. Now the dispenser is toward the left.

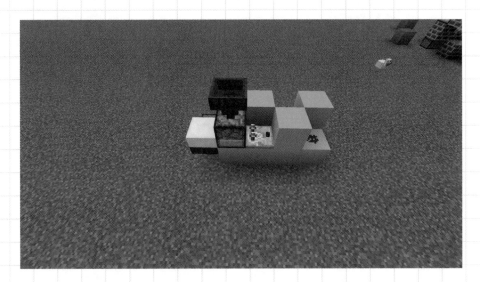

12. Place a stack of 2 blocks in front of the redstone on the right. To the left of the stack, place a single block. On top of this, place a repeater facing left.

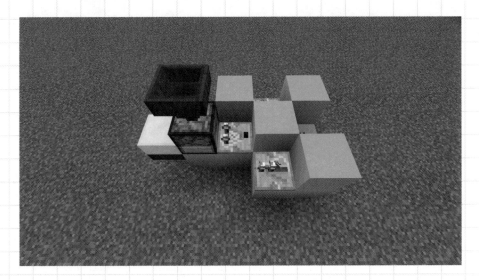

13. To the left of the repeater, place another single block, then place redstone on top. This last bit of redstone sends a signal to the comparator. The comparator, unlike a repeater, can receive signals from its two sides.

Now, if you still have the 15 eggs in the dispenser left over from your stack of test eggs, the comparator will be reactivated again and again until the eggs are thrown from the dispenser's inventory. You may see some chicks!

Each time the comparator is activated, two signals are sent: 1 signal is sent to the dispenser (along the redstone trail we created in Steps 8–10), and the second is sent back to the comparator to activate again. When the inventory behind the comparator is empty, it will no longer activate and the two signals will no longer be sent.

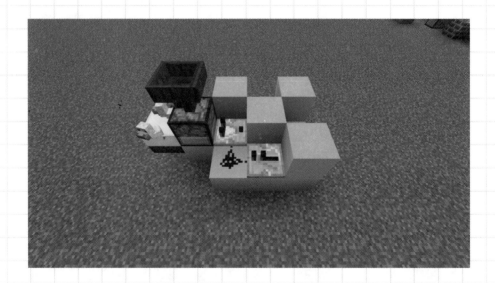

14. So we have our mechanism to collect and throw chicken eggs. We also need a mechanism to place a bucket of lava very quickly and retract it. For a dispenser to do this action, it needs to be sent 2 signals, or pulses. The first will place the lava, and the second will pick it back up again.

For the lava placement to be quick, we'll need two quick pulses. We will use a dispenser double pulse circuit. There's an explanation on how this works later in this chapter, on page 116. You can also refer to the technical diagram on page ACC-1 (page 117) for the placement of blocks in this circuit. For now, place 2 blocks next to the quartz slab where the baby chickens will hatch.

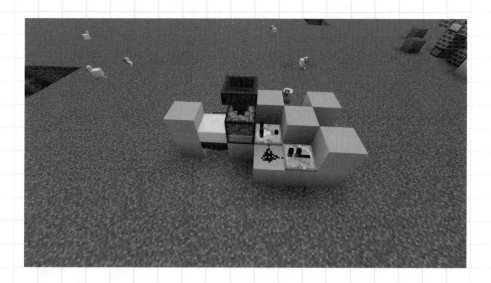

15. On top of these blocks, place a dispenser facing toward the slab.

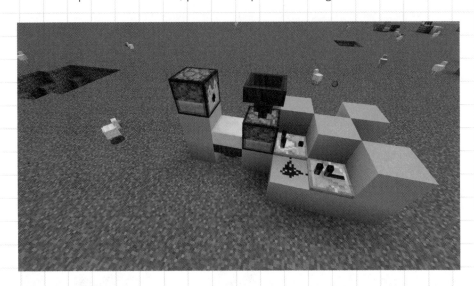

16. Place 2 blocks to the left of the dispenser and 1 to the right.

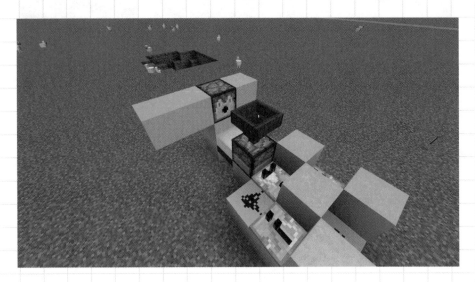

17. To the left of the 2 blocks you placed in Step 15, place a sticky piston facing up. Place another 2 blocks to the left of it, as shown.

18. Place a block above the piston. Place redstone above the 2 farthest left blocks, as shown.

19. Place a repeater to the right of the block above the piston, facing away from the piston.

20. Add 1 redstone to the right of the repeater.

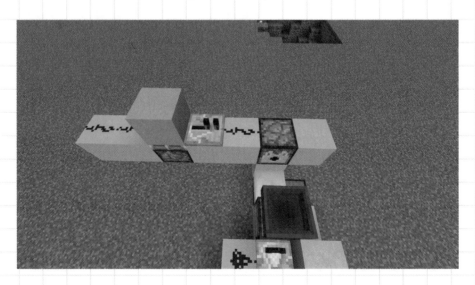

21. Place another repeater above the dispenser, also facing away from the piston. Right-click the second repeater once to add a 1-tick delay.

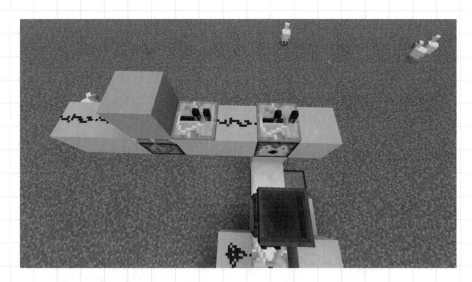

22. Add a single redstone to the right of the second repeater.

23. It's time to connect this pulse circuit to the signal from the egg dispenser. This way, whenever an egg is thrown, the circuit will dispense lava once, quickly. If there are any grown chickens in the hatching area, they will be cooked. To connect these circuits, simply run redstone from the redstone next to the comparator to the leftmost redstone in the pulse circuit. This line of redstone is shown on top of the blue blocks placed below.

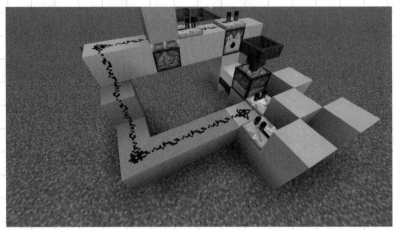

24. Now we'll need to confine the areas where the egg-laying chickens will stay. Add a 2-block-high wall above the hopper, as shown with the blue blocks below. Add up to 24 chickens into this space. (Only 24 entities are allowed to inhabit the same block.)

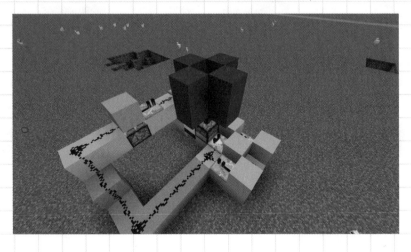

25. Next, add walls around the hatching area. I've used glass so we can see what is happening in the hatching area. Also, glass above the chest allows the chest to still open.

26. Finally, place a bucket of lava into the dispenser at the end of the pulse circuit.

27. Your chicken cooker is complete! Create a structure around it to keep it safe from accidental water spills or creeper infestation. As you can see in the chapter-opening image, I've made a structure using red bricks and jungle wood planks and slabs.

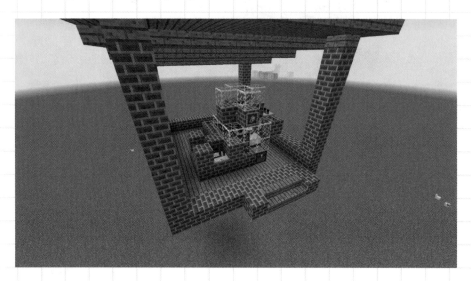

What's a Dispenser Double Pulse Circuit?

A MINECRAFT CIRCUIT IS A SET OF COMPONENTS THAT PERFORMS A SPECIFIC FUNCTION. FOR EXAMPLE, THEY MAY COMPARE TWO TYPES OF INPUTS AND THEN OUTPUT A SIGNAL DEPENDING ON WHAT THE INPUTS WERE, OR OUTPUT A SIGNAL EVERY 10 SECONDS.

A PULSE CIRCUIT CHANGES A STANDARD REDSTONE PULSE TO BE SHORTER OR LONGER, OR CHANGES IT INTO MULTIPLE PULSES. THE TYPE OF PULSE WE WANT IS 2 FAST PULSES, 1 RIGHT AFTER THE OTHER, IN ORDER TO MAKE A DISPENSER ACTIVATE TWICE QUICKLY. THIS

CIRCUIT IS A DISPENSER DOUBLE PULSER. IT SENDS A DOUBLE PULSE TO A DISPENSER.

IN THE DISPENSER DOUBLE PULSER SHOWN BELOW, THE REDSTONE PULSE COMES FROM THE LEFT, VIA A BUTTON. THE SIGNAL PASSES THROUGH THE OPAQUE BLOCK (THE GREEN ONE ON THE PISTON), BECAUSE A REPEATER IS ON THE OTHER SIDE. THE SIGNAL ALSO ACTIVATES THE STICKY PISTON, WHICH RAISES THE GREEN BLOCK. ONCE

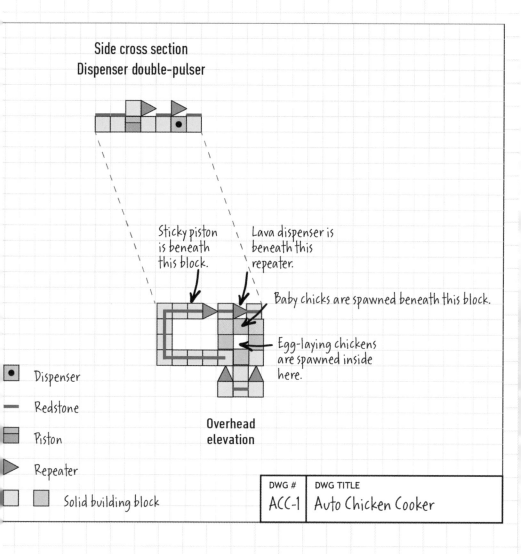

Side cross section
Dispenser double-pulser

Sticky piston is beneath this block.

Lava dispenser is beneath this repeater.

Baby chicks are spawned beneath this block.

Egg-laying chickens are spawned inside here.

Overhead elevation

- [•] Dispenser
- — Redstone
- [ ] Piston
- ▷ Repeater
- [ ] [ ] Solid building block

DWG #	DWG TITLE
ACC-1	Auto Chicken Cooker

THIS HAPPENS, THE SIGNAL IS CUT OFF IMMEDIATELY.
A STONE BUTTON SIGNAL LASTS 1.5 SECONDS. NOW THE
PULSE WILL BE MUCH SHORTER. THE SHORT PULSE
CONTINUES THROUGH TO THE NEXT REPEATER. THIS
ACTIVATES THE DISPENSER, WHICH DISPENSES WATER
OR WHATEVER ELSE YOU HAVE IN IT. THE REPEATER
IS SET TO A 1-TICK DELAY, SO IT ALSO DELAYS THE
PULSE THAT PASSES THROUGH IT TO THE NEXT BLOCK.
BECAUSE THE PULSE IS SO SHORT, THE FIRST PULSE
THAT ACTIVATED THE DISPENSER IS OVER BY THE TIME
THE SIGNAL REACHES THE LAST BIT OF REDSTONE ON
THE FAR RIGHT. THIS THEN ACTIVATES THE DISPENSER
AGAIN. IF A BUCKET OF WATER IS POURED BY THE FIRST
ACTIVATION, IT'S PICKED UP QUICKLY HERE.

CHAPTER 8
WHAT'S NEXT?

CONGRATULATIONS ON BECOMING A MINECRAFTER ENGINEER!

After building these farms, you are well on your way to managing the most challenging gameplay of Minecraft—making working contraptions using Minecraft physics and redstone energy.

There are a few steps you can take now to keep learning about redstone and making farms and contraptions.

1. First, copy and follow what other players have built. On YouTube, you will find lots of players of different abilities sharing their contraptions. Find some that you like and rebuild these, looking at what each redstone element is doing. You can try to figure out what each element or section is doing by building a contraption in parts and testing to see what it does.

2. Second, try making your own contraptions. Start very simple: Open doors and move blocks around. You may have an idea for improving or customizing some of the starter farms in this book, or they may inspire you to do something totally different. If you have an idea of what you want to do, but your redstone just isn't working right, you can search online to see what other people have done to solve the problem.

3. Most importantly, keep practicing. Making mistakes and figuring them out is the best way to learn and to get inspiration. Even if you don't understand exactly how something works, keep at it, copying other builds and trying to see how they work. Your mind will continue working "behind the scenes" as you practice, and one day it will just click!

If you like the idea of making technical drawings of your designs, you can easily make them using square-gridded (quadrille or graph) paper and colored markers and pencils.

Have fun, and share your creations!